Amelia Earhart

TAMRA B. ORR

Children's Press®
An Imprint of Scholastic Inc.
New York Toronto London Auckland Sydney
Mexico City New Delhi Hong Kong
Danbury, Connecticut

Content Consultant
James Marten, PhD
Professor and Chair, History Department
Marquette University
Milwaukee, Wisconsin

Library of Congress Cataloging-in Publication Data
Orr, Tamra, author.
 Amelia Earhart / by Tamra B. Orr.
   pages cm. — (A true book)
 Summary: "Learn about the life and accomplishments of Amelia Earhart"— Provided by publisher.
 Audience: Age 9–12.
 Audience: Grades 4–6.
 Includes bibliographical references and index.
 ISBN 978-0-531-21193-9 (library binding : alk. paper) — ISBN 978-0-531-21207-3 (pbk. : alk. paper)
 1. Earhart, Amelia, 1897-1937—Juvenile literature. 2. Women air pilots—United States—
Biography—Juvenile literature. 3. Air pilots—United States—Biography—Juvenile literature. I.
Title. II. Series: True book.
 TL540.E3O77 2015
 629.13092—dc23   2014030977

© 2015 Scholastic Inc.
All rights reserved. Published in 2015 by Children's Press, an imprint of Scholastic Inc. Published
simultaneously in Canada. Printed in China 62.
SCHOLASTIC, CHILDREN'S PRESS, A TRUE BOOK™ and associated logos are trademarks and/or
registered trademarks of Scholastic Inc.
1 2 3 4 5 6 7 8 9 10 R 24 23 22 21 20 19 18 17 16 15

**Front cover: Earhart in Hawaii before
leaving for California in 1935**

**Back cover: Earhart in an
experimental glider in 1929**

Find the Truth!

Everything you are about to read is true *except* for one of the sentences on this page.

Which one is **TRUE**?

T or F Amelia Earhart did not always plan to be a pilot.

T or F Amelia Earhart's plane was found in the middle of the Pacific Ocean.

Find the answers in this book.

3

Contents

THE BIG TRUTH!

In Good Company

Early pilots often made
careers of doing stunts,
testing new planes, and
entering competitions.

4

Earhart looked and dressed like her male pilot friends.

**The entire world wanted
to know what happened to
Amelia after she disappeared.**

CHAPTER 1

A Spirit of Adventure

Young Amelia stopped and stared. The 1904 World's Fair in St. Louis, Missouri, was the most incredible place she had ever been. She soared up to the sky in a Ferris wheel. She rode on the back of a slow, gentle elephant. Then she spotted the huge wooden roller coaster. She watched as the cars went impossibly fast along the track. They swayed, turned, and plummeted down before racing back up to the top.

The Ferris wheel was named for its inventor, George Washington Gale Ferris.

A Need for Speed

Amelia Earhart had never seen anything so wonderful! Unfortunately, her parents would not let her go on the ride. She was not about to give up, though. She wanted to know what it was like to ride a roller coaster, so she decided to make her own. Together with her younger sister, Muriel, and their cousin Ralphie, Amelia began building a ride in her grandparents' backyard.

Muriel nicknamed her sister Meelie.

Muriel (left) and Amelia Earhart pose for a picture in 1904.

The children used whatever materials were available for their roller coaster, including a simple crate.

The cousins created a rickety track, starting from the roof of the yard's toolshed. They used a wooden packing crate for the roller coaster car and greased the track with lard to make it slippery. When Amelia tried out the coaster, she went careening to the end. She slammed into the ground, tearing her dress and earning a few bruises. Amelia did not care. She said the experience was "just like flying."

Amelia's thirst for excitement continued into her adult years.

Amelia Earhart bought her first plane at age 24.

Amelia's mother was not pleased with her daughters' roller coaster adventure. The ride was soon taken apart, but it was too late. Amelia's spirit of adventure had been awakened. She was ready to find out what she could do next! Were there other ways she could learn to fly?

In the Beginning

The woman who would make history in the air was born July 24, 1897, in Atchison, Kansas. Her parents were Amy Otis Earhart and Edwin Stanton Earhart. Amy and Edwin struggled for years. Edwin moved a lot from one job to the next, from city to city, and money was often in short supply. After a second daughter, Grace Muriel, was born in 1899, the Earharts made a difficult decision. They sent Amelia to live with her grandparents on their farm.

Amelia Mary Earhart was named after her grandmothers, Amelia Otis and Mary Earhart.

Luckily, the farm was not far away—only about 50 miles (80 kilometers). It was not a hardship for Amelia because she loved being out in the country. The rest of the family came out on weekends and holidays to visit. Amelia stayed with her grandparents throughout her elementary school years. She spent her time exploring the woods, capturing insects, and having mud ball fights.

Amelia enjoyed her childhood on her grandparents' farm.

Amelia's father (left) stands with her mother (right) in Kansas City.

Amelia rejoined her parents and sister when they moved to Des Moines, Iowa, in 1909 so Edwin could take a job with a railroad line. Over the next several years, this and other jobs came and went for Edwin. His **alcoholism** also put a strain on the family. By Amelia's high school years, they lived in Chicago. Amelia had a hard time there and few friends. However, life was about to change again.

Earhart stayed at Ogontz School until 1918.

CHAPTER 2

Lessons and the Canary

High school had been difficult for Amelia Earhart. A loner, she had focused on her classes rather than on making friends or playing sports. After graduating, she enrolled at Ogontz, a finishing school in Pennsylvania where girls learned proper behavior and manners. There, she blossomed. She joined the field hockey and basketball teams. She loved her classes and earned excellent grades. She also began to think about her future.

Ogontz School was open for 100 years, closing in 1950.

Earhart was inspired by women who had jobs traditionally held by men, such as Jeannette Rankin (shown above speaking), the first woman in the U.S. Congress.

Inspiration

Newspaper clippings, photographs, and magazine articles all went into a scrapbook Earhart kept. Throughout her time at Ogontz, she collected information about women who inspired her. From American lawyers to foreign bank clerks and accountants, any woman in an important career was added to the scrapbook. She hoped that one day, she could be added to these pages.

Supporting the Troops

As the United States entered World War I in 1917, Earhart became involved in helping the troops. She knitted sweaters for the soldiers and organized a Red Cross chapter at Ogontz. The Red Cross organization supports a community's health and well-being. However, Earhart truly realized the war's impact while visiting her sister in Toronto, Canada. She saw former soldiers who had been sent home from the conflict after losing limbs, going blind, or experiencing other serious damage. It was time to do more.

More than 8.5 million people died during World War I.

At the Airfield

Earhart quit school and began working at a military hospital in Toronto. She took care of many injured officers and soldiers. In the process, she met a number of pilots. One pilot invited her and her sister to come watch him fly at a stunt-flying show at a nearby airfield. When Earhart saw the planes in the air, she was amazed. She loved the gracefulness of flight and even the risk involved.

Earhart's time as a nurse later inspired her to study medicine.

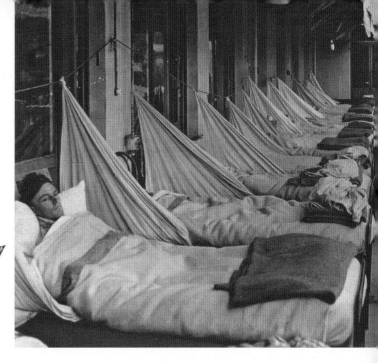

The Spanish flu killed an estimated 50 million people around the world between 1918 and 1919.

Although Earhart wanted to know more about flight, her health interfered. In late 1918, she was hospitalized with a serious sinus infection while treating patients during a deadly Spanish flu outbreak. She had surgery and spent months recovering. In the meantime, she tried to decide what to do with her future. She took a course in automobile engine repair. A year later, she enrolled in Columbia University to study medicine. However, Earhart soon left the university.

Earhart was partially inspired to fly by seeing stunt pilots perform daring, dangerous feats.

An Important Ride

In late 1920, Earhart took her first plane ride at California's Daugherty Field and was hooked. On January 3, 1921, she had her first flight lesson at Kinner Field. Earhart soon purchased a Kinner Airster. Bert Kinner, who owned Kinner Field, produced the plane. Earhart paid for it with savings and by working as a clerk and gravel truck driver. She named the bright yellow plane *The Canary*.

Anita Snook

Over time, Earhart became close with her first flight teacher, Anita "Neta" Snook. Snook, or "Snooky" as she was known, was a great choice for Earhart. Although she was only 24 years old, Snooky had already bought and learned to rebuild her own biplane. She earned a living giving flying lessons, doing **aerial** advertising and **barnstorming**, taking visitors for city tours by air, and test-flying planes.

In Good Company

Flying was considered "unfeminine," and people tried to discourage Amelia Earhart from taking part in it. However, even in the early days of flight, she was not the only woman in a plane. Here are a few other female flyers who made their mark on history.

Raymonde de Laroche, the daughter of a plumber, grew up in France interested in cars, motorcycles, and acting. In 1909, she became the first woman in the world to fly a plane solo. The next year, she became the first woman to earn a pilot's license.

Bessica Raiche was a pioneer for women in medicine. She also made history for women in flight. In 1910, she became the first American woman to fly a plane solo. She and her husband had built her aircraft themselves out of silk, piano wire, and bamboo.

Harriet Quimby was a journalist before becoming interested in flight. In 1911, she became the first woman in the United States—and the second woman in the world—to earn a pilot's license. She was also the first woman to fly at night and to fly solo across the English Channel.

Bessie Coleman became the first African American, man or woman, to earn a pilot's license, in 1921. Not allowed to learn in the United States, she moved to France to take flying lessons. She returned to the United States with her license and became a successful barnstormer.

24

CHAPTER 3

Fame, Fortune, and Danger

Learning to fly, Earhart was on her way to becoming the celebrity she is remembered as today. The media eventually noticed her, and the loner from high school was soon called a "society girl-student **aviatrix**" by the newspapers. Adding to her popularity, Earhart had a unique fashion style. She wore a leather helmet, goggles, **jodhpurs**, a tie, and a long leather coat and looked like a flying **ace**.

Goggles protected a pilot's eyes from the wind in planes whose cockpits were open to the air.

Gaining Confidence

To add to her look, Earhart began cutting her hair. At first, she just cut off short pieces of hair so her mother would not notice. Eventually, she had it cut into a short style called a bob.

By working multiple jobs, Earhart was able to pay for her expensive flight lessons. She learned to do stunts such as loops, barrel rolls, dives, and tailspins. Each one gave her more confidence as a pilot.

Earhart's short hair became one of her most recognizable features.

Earhart sold her first plane to finance her family's trip across the country.

Changing Times

Earhart's skill grew. She earned her pilot's license and set a world record, flying higher than any woman had before. But while life was exciting, it was not without troubles. At one point, Earhart sold her Airster to help her parents financially. When her parents divorced, she moved her mother and sister to the East Coast. Throughout this time, Earhart's sinuses continued to bother her. She had to have additional surgeries years after her illness in 1918.

Though flying was a big part of her life while living in California, Earhart had largely given up flight after moving to Massachusetts.

In autumn 1926, Earhart found another passion. She was hired as an assistant at the Denison House, a **settlement house** in Boston, Massachusetts. She helped immigrants learn English, led games for the children, and took families to and from their medical appointments. By 1928, she had joined the board of directors.

With no plane of her own, Earhart was flying less. Was her career in flying over? The answer came from two unexpected directions.

First, Bert Kinner asked Earhart to help him sell his planes on the East Coast. Earhart agreed. She helped him scout sites for his future airport and find customers for his products.

Second, Charles Lindbergh made international headlines in spring 1927 when he became the first person to fly solo across the Atlantic Ocean. Suddenly, the entire world was more interested in flying—including Earhart.

Lindbergh's flight across the Atlantic Ocean lasted 33.5 hours.

A Rocky Trial Run

In spring 1928, Earhart was asked to be a passenger on an Atlantic flight imitating Lindbergh's journey. How could she say no? She kept the flight a secret, writing letters to her parents and creating a will just in case.

The trip was difficult! The crew coped with a broken door lock, an oil tank leak, unexpected fog, a malfunctioning radio, engine trouble, and stormy weather.

Earhart later described her role on the 1928 flight as being "just baggage, like a sack of potatoes."

In 1928, crowds gather in Southampton in the United Kingdom to welcome the *Friendship* and its crew.

Though only a passenger, Earhart received a great deal of international attention for being the first woman to cross the Atlantic in a plane. She was nicknamed Lady Lindy and soon wrote a book about the historic flight.

Earhart's pathway in life was clear now: she would spend it flying. She bought a new Lockheed Vega plane and focused on showing the world what a determined woman could do!

CHAPTER 4

Around the World

Earhart kept flying and setting records. She also went on lecture tours. In 1931, she married her manager, G. P. Putnam. The following year, she wrote an autobiography about her adventures in the air.

In the spring of 1932, Amelia announced she was going to fly across the Atlantic—this time, as the pilot. She spent months preparing. She improved her plane and took lessons on how to "fly blind," or rely on instrument readings alone.

Earhart met Putnam when he hired her for the 1928 flight across the Atlantic Ocean.

Earhart's 1932 flight across the Atlantic Ocean lasted less than 15 hours.

Trouble in the Air

Earhart's flight lasted less than a day but was difficult. First, her **altimeter** failed. Then she noticed a fire in the engine. When she flew higher to avoid storms, her wings and windshield iced over. This sent her plummeting toward the ocean in a spin. She pulled out of it just in time. She also ran into fog. Finally, she switched on her reserve gas tank and discovered a fuel leak. Earhart ended up making an emergency landing in a pasture in Northern Ireland.

Although she was forced to land earlier than planned, Earhart still completed the longest and fastest nonstop flight in history. Well known before, Earhart was now famous. When she returned to New York City, she was met with a **ticker tape** parade and an air show by the army, navy, and air force. She received several medals and had dinner with President Herbert Hoover at the White House.

Earhart (holding flowers) is honored for her historic flight, at a ceremony in New York City in June 1932.

First Ladies and Fashion

In 1933, Earhart had dinner with the newly elected president Franklin D. Roosevelt and his wife, Eleanor. Earhart was delighted when the first lady asked to fly over Washington, D.C., at night. Amelia agreed. Both still dressed in their silk evening gowns, the women climbed aboard a Condor airplane and took off. When they returned, they hopped in Earhart's car and took a drive around the White House grounds.

Eleanor Roosevelt obtained a student's flying permit after flying with Earhart.

Earhart talks with young students about flight.

The following year, Earhart launched her own clothing line called Amelia Fashions. Geared for "the woman who lives actively," the clothing was sold in department stores in New York City and Chicago, Illinois.

Earhart spent most of her time traveling and giving lectures. However, she knew it was time for a new challenge.

Earhart poses next to her new Lockheed Electra.

Earhart planned to follow the equator, the longest route around the world.

A Grand Finale

Earhart had an idea. She wanted to fly around the world solo. It would be her last professional flight. Earhart's flight would be considered "solo" because she would do all the actual flying. One companion, Fred Noonan, would navigate and work the radio. Using money she earned as a consultant for Purdue University, she bought a new Lockheed 10E Electra. It would be her last plane.

Earhart's flight was going to be immense, and her plane required thousands of dollars of improvements before the journey. To lighten the plane, she removed the Morse code equipment and long-distance radio antenna. Later, she also took out the parachutes. All of those decisions seemed logical but may have been fatal mistakes. In February 1937, Amelia announced her flight plans to the world.

Earhart and Noonan inspect their plane.

A Flight Into Mystery

On launch day in March, the plane's landing gear collapsed and a wing was torn. The flight was postponed three months for repairs. By the time the plane was ready, the flight faced new challenges. The entire route had to be changed to avoid possible **monsoons**. Finally, on June 1, 1937, Earhart and Noonan took off from Miami.

As Earhart flew, she sent logbooks and notes home. The world followed her journey on the radio and news.

Timeline of Earhart's Life

1897
Amelia Earhart is born in Atchison, Kansas.

1920
Earhart takes her first ride in an airplane.

Everywhere Earhart and Noonan landed, they were welcomed warmly. Although they encountered bad weather and had equipment malfunctions, the flight was generally a success.

By day 30, there were only two more stops before returning home. On July 2, the plane left the tiny runway in Lae, New Guinea. Multiple ships were stationed to guide Earhart 2,556 miles (4,113 km) to her destination, Howland Island in the Pacific Ocean. Tragically, Earhart's last hours were plagued with communication problems.

1937
Earhart and Fred Noonan attempt to fly around the world.

1932
Earhart becomes the first woman to fly solo across North America and back and to fly across the Atlantic.

Radio transmissions were garbled. Two-way communication was impossible. Earhart's last message came in hours after she was supposed to have landed. She must have been dangerously low on fuel. She sounded frantic and lost. Then—silence.

An intense search continued for two weeks. It covered hundreds of thousands of square miles but found nothing. The beloved pilot was gone. She left behind a reminder that life is an adventurous ride, full of risk and reward.

Earhart's disappearance shocked the public.

The Search Continues

Almost 80 years after Earhart went missing, the search for her continues. Many organizations have taken teams out to search for plane wreckage or any other evidence of what might have happened. A number of these groups believe that she and Noonan landed on the uninhabited Gardner Island, now called Nikumaroro, and lived there as castaways. Perhaps one day the mystery will be solved. ★

Year Earhart earned her pilot's license: 1923

Date the U.S. Post Office issued an Amelia Earhart stamp: July 24, 1963

Date Earhart went missing: July 2, 1937

Date Earhart was officially declared dead: January 5, 1939

Amount the U.S. government spent searching for Earhart: $4 million, or about $56 million in today's dollars, more than any other search before it

Distance Earhart traveled in her journey around the world before disappearing: More than 22,000 mi. (35,406 km), or about two-thirds of the trip

Year Earhart received the National Geographic Society's Gold Medal: 1932

Year Earhart received the U.S. Distinguished Flying Cross: 1932, the first woman to do so

Did you find the truth?

Amelia Earhart did not always plan to be a pilot.

Amelia Earhart's plane was found in the middle of the Pacific Ocean.

Resources

Books

Fleming, Candace. *Amelia Lost: The Life and Disappearance of Amelia Earhart*. New York: Schwartz & Wade, 2011.

Freedman, Lew. *All About Amelia Earhart*. Indianapolis, IN: Blue River Press, 2014.

Gilpin, Caroline. *Amelia Earhart*. Washington, DC: National Geographic, 2013.

Visit this Scholastic Web site for more information on Amelia Earhart:
★ www.factsfornow.scholastic.com
Enter the keywords **Amelia Earhart**

Important Words

ace (AYS) — someone who is an expert at something, particularly flying

aerial (AIR-ee-uhl) — happening in the air

alcoholism (AL-kuh-hawl-ism) — the state of being unable to stop the habit of drinking too much alcohol

altimeter (al-TIM-i-tur) — an instrument that measures how high something is above the ground

aviatrix (ay-vee-AY-triks) — a female pilot

barnstorming (BARN-stor-ming) — giving exhibitions of stunt flying or races for an audience

jodhpurs (JAHD-purz) — riding pants that are full over the hips and narrow from the knees to the ankles

monsoons (mahn-SOONZ) — very strong winds that occur in different parts of the world; in summer, the winds blow from the ocean, causing heavy rains; in winter, they blow toward the ocean, creating hot, dry weather

settlement house (SET-uhl-muhnt HOWS) — an inner-city institution that provides educational, recreational, and social services to a community

ticker tape (TIK-ur TAYP) — long, thin pieces of paper on which news is printed by a special machine, called a ticker; often torn up and used as confetti during parades

Index

Page numbers in **bold** indicate illustrations.

About the Author

Tamra B. Orr is the author of hundreds of books for readers of all ages. She has a degree in English and secondary education from Ball State University, and now lives in the Pacific Northwest. She is the mother of four children and loves to spend her free time reading, writing, and going camping. She is fascinated by strong, brave, and imaginative women such as Amelia Earhart. Like countless others, she hopes that one day the news will report Earhart actually landed on an island and died at a very old age, leaving behind her children, grandchildren, and great-grandchildren.